MALLARDS

MALLARDS

Text and Photographs by
Scott Nielsen

Voyageur Press

Printed in Hong Kong
92 93 94 95 96 5 4 3 2 1

Library of Congress Cataloging-in-Publication Data

Nielsen, Scott.
Mallards / text and photography by Scott Nielsen.
p. cm.
Includes index.
ISBN 0-89658-172-1
1. Mallard. 2. Mallard—Pictorial works. I. Title.
QL696.A52N54 1992
598.4'1—dc20
91-40858
CIP

Published by
Voyageur Press, Inc.
P.O. Box 338, 123 North Second Street
Stillwater, MN 55082 U.S.A.
From Minnesota and Canada 612-430-2210
Toll-free 800-888-9653

Voyageur Press books are also available at discounts for quantities for
educational, fundraising, premium, or sales-promotion use. For
details contact the marketing department. Please write or call for our
free catalog of natural history publications.

Front cover: *This is the photo I've entitled "Exploding Into Spring." In the photo, a drake mallard in full breeding plumage takes to the air, leaving in his wake a splash of water. I always try to get the sun in my photos, because it is the source of life's vitality and energy. In this case, the sun is a reflection in the bird's eye plus reflections from the hundreds of droplets he's kicked up.*

Back cover: *One-week-old mallard ducklings.*

Page 3: *Mallards make a variety of vocalizations such as whistlelike calls and nasal tones, but by far the most familiar is the "quack." Male voices are usually lower in pitch than female voices.*

Page 144: *A hen mallard and her two-week-old ducklings soak up the midmorning sun only twenty yards from the front door of my home.*

In order to see birds it is necessary to become a part of the silence. One has to sit still like a mystic and wait. One soon learns that fussing, instead of achieving things, merely prevents things from happening.

Robert Lund, "Solomon in All His Glory"

Contents

Introduction

With camera in hand, I floated a scant ten feet from this wild mallard, enabling me to show the bird from a mallard's-eye view, the perspective I think shows them best.

Mallards are normally wary birds, but it seemed that I attracted this drake's curiosity, if mallards have such a trait. In this picture, I got just the right combination of wariness and curiosity. If I had been any closer to the bird, he would have been long gone; any farther away and he probably wouldn't have paid any attention to me.

Introduction

At first glance, this is a book about my experiences with the particular group of mallards that calls my Northwoods lake its home. But in addition, *Mallards* is a fitting description of this species throughout its range—the Northern Hemisphere—because the mallard's behavior and chronology of nesting is virtually the same throughout. With a few changes in background vegetation, the photographs could just as easily be of mallards in a London park, a Siberian river, a Japanese garden, or an Australian marsh.

I look at this photo collection not as an example of my knowledge of photography, which I consider minimal, but rather as testimony to an understanding of the birds themselves. But to share my understanding, I have started with these photographs. All of the images are of live, noncaptive birds photographed in the wild under natural, unmanipulated conditions. Most were taken with only a 300-mm lens at distances of thirteen to twenty-five feet; occasionally I was as little as six feet from my wild prey.

Learning about my subject, anticipating the situations I'll find myself in, perfecting my technique so that I can instead concentrate on the birds themselves and what they have to teach me: These are the things I most enjoy about my work with nature. Sometimes I outsmart the birds, and other times they fool me, but the experience is enjoyable even if I don't come back with tangible results. Fishing is not necessarily about catching fish, hunting doesn't always mean harvesting game, and photography is about a lot more than taking pictures.

Photography allows me to step outside myself. We tend to impose our human perspectives on everything around us, but with a camera I can instead visualize birds as others of their species see them. It is from this nonhuman

The mallard's name is derived from the old French maslard, *meaning "wild drake," or* mallart, *meaning "male duck." The female is pictured at left; the male is above.*

I watched a drake burst into flight, and for an instant I followed along. Mallards are at home in all the elements of air, water, and land, but it's during the transition from one element to another (in this case, water to air) that I think they are most beautiful.

viewpoint, I believe, that birds are the most beautiful. I hinted at this concept in my previous book, *A Season with Eagles,* where I mentioned setting up my blind in such a way as to give me an eagle's eyesight and perspective. *Mallards* elaborates on this idea. If the ducks were on the water, I was floating with them; if they were on the ground, I was lying nearby; and if they were in the air, as much as possible I was flying alongside.

Although I have a fair amount of formal training in ornithology, at no point in the text did I limit myself to writing about what you can read in scientific journals and hefty biological monographs. We will never know all the details of why birds do what they do. Most of it is probably instinctive, but I'm fascinated by the seeming logic of what they do and the simple, straightforward means they use to deal with the situations they face. I've included as much insight as I can into the mallard's behavior and lifestyle, even if some thoughts haven't been scientifically proven.

What you have in your hands, then, is my understanding of the mallard, or, more properly, a translation of that understanding into words and pictures. As with all translations, something is lost in the process, and I hope you take this book not as the final word on mallards, but rather as an example of what one inquisitive person can do. Consider this book an invitation and encouragement to find your own special part of nature. Make the time to interact with nature using whatever tools with which you feel most comfortable, and in the process, come to a unique understanding of just how special our natural world is and how you as an individual fit into the overall picture.

The webbed toes of a mallard's orange feet enable it to swim easily through the water.

Mallards

When mention is made of ducks, you probably first think of the mallard, and for many good reasons. The mallard's adaptability has helped make it the Northern Hemisphere's most common and widespread waterfowl species. All domestic forms of ducks, except the Muscovy, are descended from the wild mallard, which was first tamed by the Romans in pre-Christian times as a source of meat and eggs, much like the wild junglefowl was domesticated to become our present-day chicken. Most standard duck calls are patterned after the distinctive *quack* of the mallard. The drake's nicknames "greenhead" and "curly-tail" refer to parts of its plumage that most everyone incorrectly visualizes as belonging to all ducks. And perhaps the mallard is best known because the adaptability of the female when nesting has made her as much at home in city parks and golf courses as in isolated marshes. Rare is the season when the national media does not feature photos and stories of mallard hens and their newly hatched broods negotiating clogged city streets on their way from nest site to foraging area.

The cosmopolitan mallard (*Anas platyrhynchos*) is the most abundant member of the waterfowl family (*Anatidae*) of birds, which comprises about 150 species of ducks, geese, and swans. Although the waterfowl range in size from the thirty-pound swan to the teal and others weighing less than a pound, the mallard typifies many of the natural adaptations that it shares with its near and distant cousins: The mallard is adapted for a primarily aquatic lifestyle; the toes of its orange feet are webbed for swimming in the water; it is a strong flyer, whether in hopping from one pond to another in search of food or in migrating thousands of miles; and a dense layer of feathers (the full-grown mallard has about 10,000 feathers) and fat helps insulate the mallard against

A mallard drake is a spectrum in motion. The iridescent green feathers on his head include the ear coverts.
(Coverts refers to small feathers that cover the bases of larger feathers, or in the case of the ear coverts,
feathers that cover the ear opening.) On his wings are the eye-catching purple secondary feathers (also
known as the speculum feathers). Also on the wings are the more mutely colored primaries—large feathers
at the tip of the wing, the tertials, the scapulars, and wing coverts.

The drake mallard is the only species of duck worldwide to have curled undertail coverts, although many people mistakenly assume these coverts are found in all male ducks.

This three-pound drake mallard floats alongside an eighteen-pound tundra swan, one of the largest species of waterfowl.

wind and cold temperatures. Waterfowl regularly apply a layer of oil to these feathers for waterproofing. All waterfowl hatch precocial young, birds capable of leaving the nest and feeding themselves within a day of hatching. Waterfowl parents attend to the young and provide protection against predators and the weather, but they do not feed their offspring directly.

But mallards and most ducks also differ from their distant cousins. While males and females of the geese and swan species mate for life and raise their young together, duck individuals generally find new mates each year, and most duck drakes (males) desert their hens (females) during incubation. Geese males and females have virtually identical plumages, as do swan males and females, but each species of ducks displays noticeable differences in feathering between the sexes, a phenomenon known as sexual dimorphism. The drake mallard's eye-catching, metallic green head is fine for attracting a mate each spring, but his bright feathering would be a liability when raising young because, in comparison to the well-camouflaged hen, it would likely attract predators.

Members of the waterfowl family vary in their diets and methods of food gathering. The much-loved Canada goose often feeds grain left lying in fields, while the common loon feeds on fish and aquatic insects. Food-gathering methods also vary among the different species of ducks, and these different methods loosely categorize all ducks into one of two groups: diving or dabbling ducks (see also page *44*). Diving ducks, such as the canvasback, ringneck, bufflehead, and goldeneye, submerge themselves beneath the water when searching for food, which can be either plants or animal matter, such as clams, snails, and insects. Diving ducks are heavy-bodied, and the divers have relatively small, narrow wings, improving their diving capabilities. However, the smaller wings compromise their ability to quickly take flight, and, except in a strong headwind that fills their

The distinctive quack, glistening green head, and curled black undertail coverts unquestionably identify this bird as a mallard drake—even to the neophyte bird-watchers among us.

This hen is using her bill to collect oil from the opening of the preen gland at the base of her tail. Once on the bill, the oil is applied to the feathers for waterproofing.

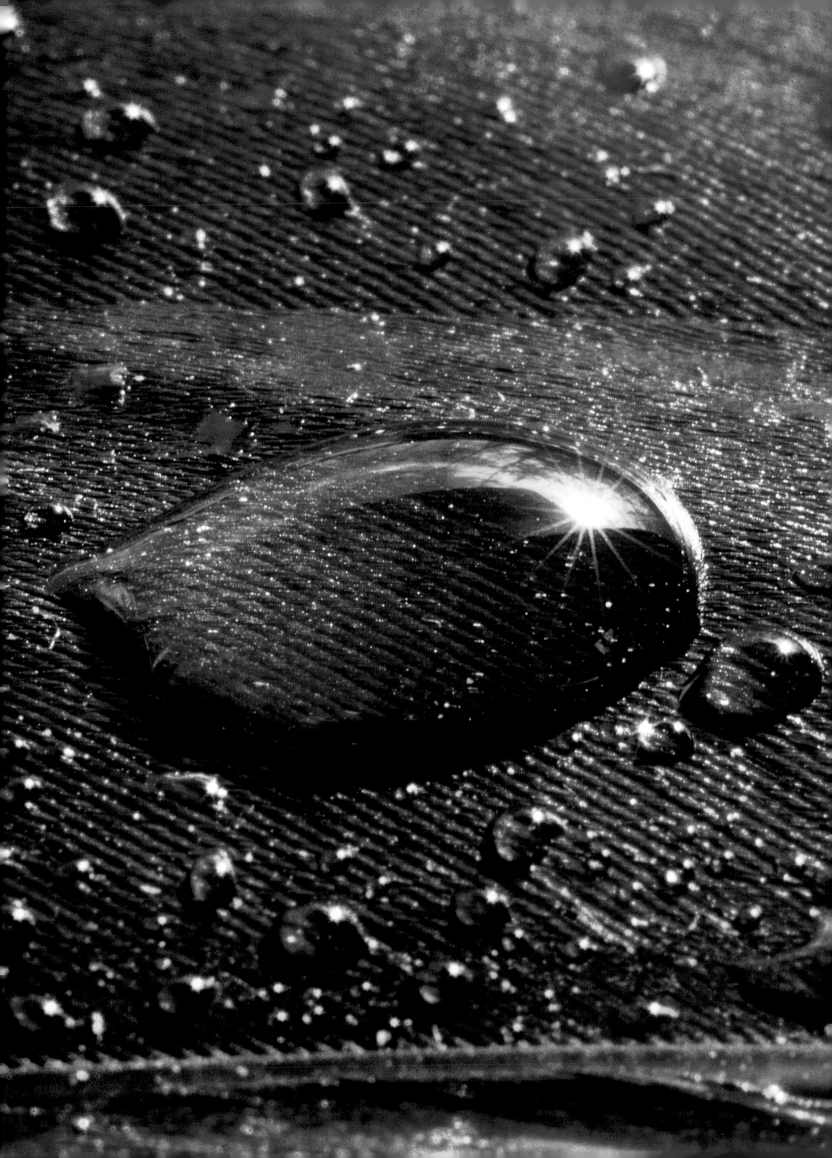

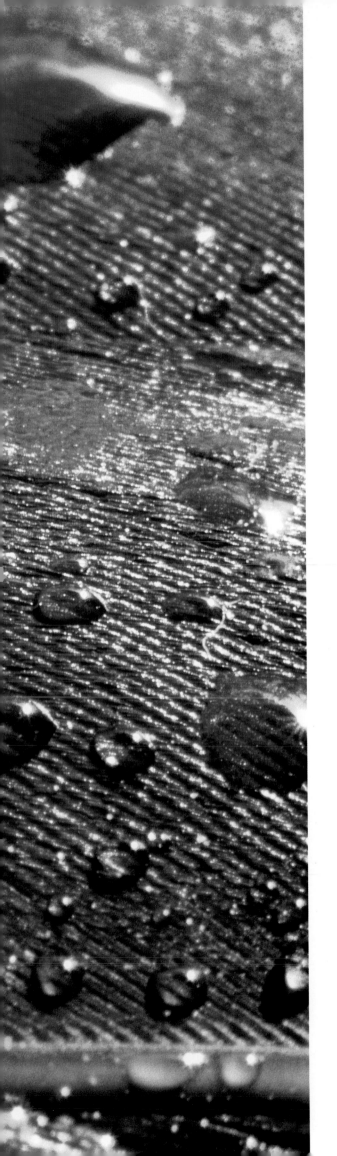

Waterproofing is so good in ducks that liquids bead up on the feathers rather than soaking in, as shown by these wing feathers. The blue feathers in the photo at left are the bird's speculum feathers.

Once hatching is complete, the hen keeps
a lookout for predators. She also leads her
ducklings to good feeding areas and broods
them should cold or damp weather arise.
These one-week-old mallard ducklings
(inset) have been off their nest for six days
and are already proficient at swimming
and feeding on their own.

The brightly colored drake contrasts with his mutely colored mate. It's all part of nature's design; hens pick whom they want as partners, and males therefore need bright colors to attract them. And because hens incubate and raise families, it's to their advantage to be camouflaged.

wings, divers must run along the water to get the needed lift for flight. The legs of diving ducks are placed well to the rear on the body, where they are most efficient for underwater propulsion, but this makes them awkward when trying to walk on land. Whoever coined the phrase "a duck out of water" must have been observing a diving duck.

Mallards are members of the dabbling duck tribe, which also includes such species as the teal, pintail, and wigeon. Although they may occasionally dive for food, most dabblers prefer to "tip-up" to reach food that is only a foot or two beneath the surface. The ground beneath these shallow water areas receives much sunlight, permitting extensive growth of vegetation, and it is not surprising that dabblers eat more plants than animal matter when compared to the divers. Because the mallard and other dabblers needn't submerge routinely to reach their food, their bodies can be more buoyant. They float higher on the water than divers do, and because they have larger wings, dabblers can usually take flight with a jump from a stationary position on the water surface or on land. Next to the wood duck, the mallard has the broadest wings in relation to its weight of any North American waterfowl species. Coupled with massive pectoral (chest) muscles to drive these wings, the mallard can explode straight up out of the water, something a diving duck could only dream of.

In comparison to a diver's legs, a dabbling duck's feet are centered beneath its body. Although still somewhat awkward on land, the dabbler can walk much more easily than the diver can when searching for food. The mallard is as much at home in feeding on corn, oats, and other cultivated grain crops as it is in searching marshes and more conventional locations.

Indeed, versatility and adaptability are the stock in trade of the mallard. Its varied diet and feeding locations, its ability to successfully nest in a variety of environments, its relative tolerance of humans: All have

The legs of diving ducks, such as the ringneck (inset), are placed toward the rear of the body, where they are more useful under water. On the ground, they must hold themselves in an upright position to keep from falling over. The legs of mallards and other dabbling ducks are centered more directly beneath their bodies—an advantage when walking on land but a disadvantage when diving.

The relatively narrow wings and heavy body of this bufflehead mean that it must run along the water surface to get the necessary liftoff speed.

In contrast to the diving ducks, the mallard and other dabbling ducks have broad wings, powerful pectoral muscles, and buoyant bodies, enabling them to rocket into the air from the water surface. The wing and tail feathers of a mallard power and steer the bird in flight, while the contour feathers of head, neck, and body provide streamlining and protection. They also help insulate this hen from water and cold.

helped the mallard keep its head above water in the face of drought and other changes that have greatly damaged the population numbers of its cousins. Counting introduced populations in New Zealand and Australia, the mallard numbers in the tens of millions worldwide, with a breeding population of six million on the North American continent alone (down from thirteen million adults in the late 1950s).

As I write these words, a late winter snowstorm is brewing outside my northern Wisconsin home, but a few of these mallards are already inching their way north toward this home I share with them. Come with me as I follow my mallards through their annual cycle of living and renewal.

This drake mallard is "tipping up" to feed while his mate stands guard. The ability of dabblers to quickly take flight from tight places allows them to feed in shallow water yet rapidly flee from danger. In contrast, this diving bufflehead drake (inset) feeds in more open water where he can have the necessary runway to take flight. More open water is generally deeper water, and this species typically feeds at depths of five to twenty feet.

This mallard is feeding on vegetation, the most common dabbler food, although he will not hesitate to consume animal matter when it is stumbled upon.

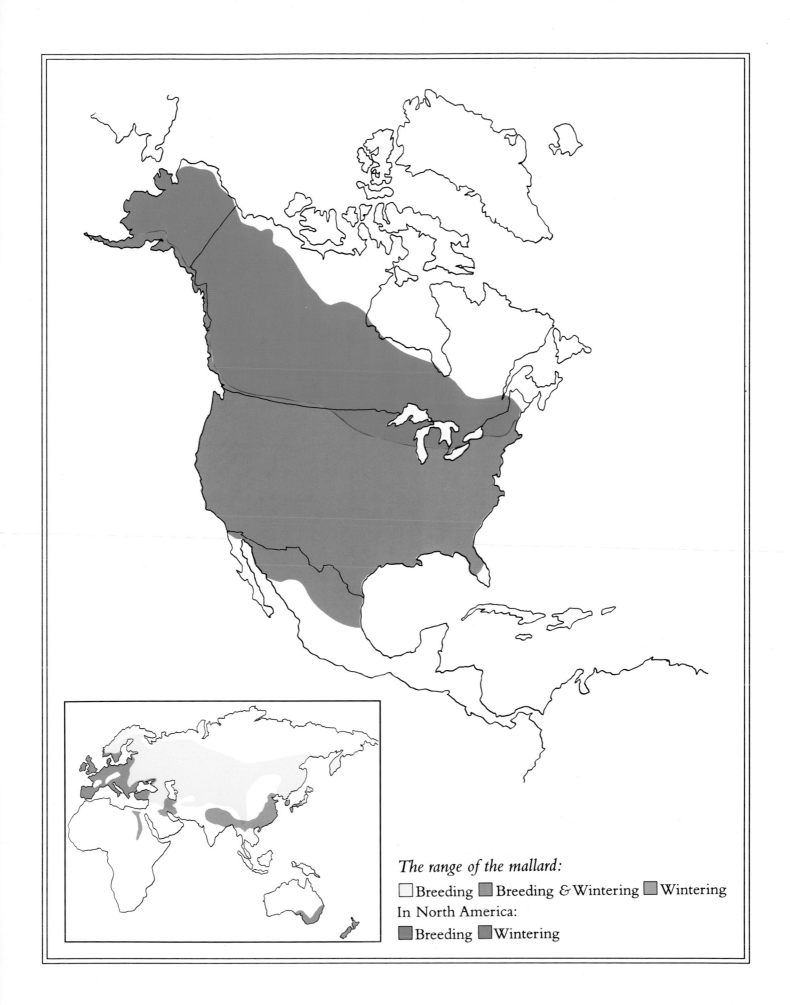

The range of the mallard:

☐ Breeding ■ Breeding & Wintering ■ Wintering

In North America:

■ Breeding ■ Wintering

The spectacular mallard ranges from Alaska and the periphery of Greenland to the southern United States and northern Mexico in North America, as well as across Eurasia, on some Atlantic islands, and as far as Australia and New Zealand. Such a vast range indicates that this is an adaptable bird—and a strong flier.

A GATHERING OF TRIBES

All ducks in the Northern Hemisphere belong to one of eight tribes: dabbling, shelduck, perching, whistling, seaduck, pochard, eider, and stifftail. The mallard is the most common member of the water-surface-feeding, or dabbler, tribe. The common shoveler is another representative; like the mallard drake, the common shoveler drake wears a proud green head, which commonly confuses bird-watchers. To distinguish the two, look for the shoveler's greatly elongated bill, a distinctive field mark.

The shelduck tribe is represented in the photos by the European shelduck. Both male and female of this species have a green head similar to the drake mallard's, although they primarily feed in shallow salt water and rarely are found more than a mile inland along European coasts.

The wood duck is probably the best known member of the perching duck tribe. As the collective name *perching* suggests, they are particularly adept at roosting in and moving among tree branches.

The fulvous whistling duck is one of the world's most widespread ducks, occurring on four continents. The whistling duck tribe is noted for its unique, whistlelike calls and extremely vocal nature. Unlike the mallard, the males and females of any particular species of whistling duck are almost identical in coloring.

All of the above four tribes are comfortable walking on land, generally stick to shallow water or fields for feeding, and have spatulate-shaped bills adapted for feeding primarily on plant matter. Together, they are loosely termed dabbling ducks, although the dabbling duck tribe is only a part of the group.

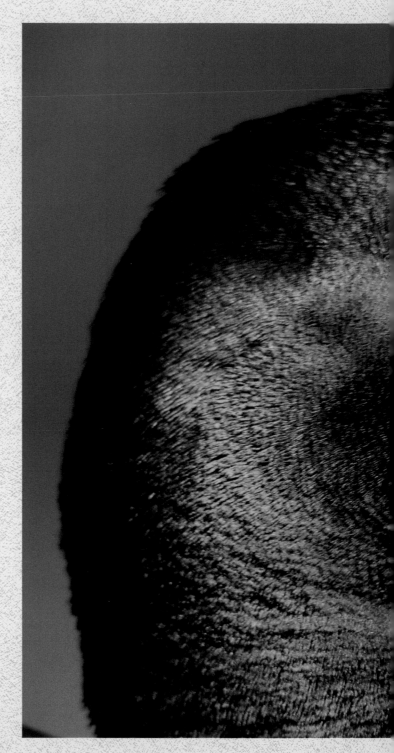

Mallard

Common shoveler

European shelduck

Fulvous whistling duck

Wood duck

The four tribes belonging to the Northern Hemisphere's group of diving ducks are the seaduck, the pochard, the eider, and the stiff-tail. The seaduck tribe varies from the fish-eating mergansers, such as the hooded merganser, with their narrow, saw-toothed bills, to the goldeneyes, with shorter, broader, heavier bills suitable for crushing the small crustaceans they are so fond of.

The pochard tribe of diving ducks is headed by the canvasback, the "king of ducks." The term divers is often used to refer specifically to the pochards, birds with compact, rounded bodies in comparison to the elongated bodies of the dabblers.

The various subspecies of common eider occur throughout the Northern Hemisphere's Arctic edges. The four species in the eider tribe are all strong divers and are just as comfortable on the ocean as on land. Eiders have strong bills for crushing mollusks, and their down is considered to be the best insulation in the world.

Stifftails are the last tribe of diving ducks. Our North American ruddy duck is perhaps the most familiar. The tails of the males are stiffly uplifted during courtship, possibly the reason for this tribe's name. Unlike most other species of ducks, male ruddys often accompany the female and her young, although he probably does not actively contribute to their care.

Hooded merganser

Canvasback

Common goldeneye

Ruddy duck

Common eider

An old hen patiently waits for the slushy ice she stands on to melt, a signal for a new nesting season.

THE RETURN

Old hens and their mates for the new season are the first mallards to arrive at the nesting area each spring. Often, the accompanying drakes are new partners, but there are cases of hens and drakes staying paired for several years. Biologists generally agree that hens return to the area of their own hatching, and drakes follow whichever hen they became paired with on the wintering grounds. Thus, a drake hatched in one area could end up in a completely different spot for nesting, one of the ways in which inbreeding is minimized. But there are exceptions to this rule. A fair number of drakes do return to the area of their birth; many of these may be unpaired surplus males who don't head north with a mate. And not all hens automatically head for their birthplace. I observed one federally banded female with her broods in northern Wisconsin for three straight years, getting close enough at times to read her band number. To my surprise, she was banded as a duckling along the Canadian border, more than 250 miles northwest of her adopted home. To further confuse things, after the hen had been coming to northwestern Wisconsin for a couple of years, a second banded hen joined her. When I sent her band number to the Bird Banding Lab in Maryland, you can imagine my surprise when they informed me that this bird was banded in the same area as the first hen, though in a different year. Perhaps the homing instinct is strongest in hens who have previously nested successfully in an area.

These mallard hens are the earliest spring waterfowl migrants in my area, usually outpacing even the pintail and goldeneye ducks as they wing their way northward. I've noted mallard pairs in the open creek by my home more than three weeks before ice left the adjacent lake along which they would later nest. Each morning and evening, the hens flew out to different locations along

This is the banded hen who nested on my lake for three straight years in spite of being hatched several hundred miles away. Thousands of ducks are banded each year; any bands recovered are sent to the federal government's banding lab in Maryland. These found bands assist biologists in censusing the population.

This hen's waiting point is a tussock of grass on a fallen log facing the lake near my home. Waiting points are used much like a ruffed grouse uses its drumming log: to communicate. From such an elevated, open location, her quacking will carry a long distance and will help keep other hens from locating too closely to her.

Any closeup portrait of a wary drake is likely to be possible because a hen rests nearby, exerting a calm on the drake. Such was the case here: An out-of-focus female is visible just behind this greenhead's bill.

These six unpaired drakes will often move about as a group in search of hens. They are unlikely to be successful when trying to mate with already paired hens, but they will be useful should any hen lose her mate.

the shore (ornithologists call them "waiting points") and quacked for several minutes to an hour. One such point, only one hundred feet from my living room window, is a tussock of grass that catches a full day's sun. The spot is usually bare of snow, even when up to a foot of it remains in nearby areas. For several years in a row, I would swear that the same hen returned to the same spot in the spring. Although not banded, her distinctive voice, more of a squeak than a quack, identified her. She ruled that roost for five years, bringing off a successful brood each year, a remarkable triumph when compared to the one or two successful nestings an average mallard hen may have in a lifetime.

Although mallards don't have a fixed territory to defend from others, possibly this "waiting-point" quacking among the old hens is a way of spreading themselves out and minimizing conflict during nesting, as there is a good correlation between waiting points and future nest locations. That is, hens commonly end up nesting near their waiting points, thereby retaining the comfortable distances from other hens that were established a week or so previously, when they vocalized to one another. Staggering, rather than grouping, the nest sites lessens the chances of a predator locating several hens' nests in one fell swoop.

Hens run the show in the spring, and drakes go wherever their mates lead them. It is during this time that I am able to get my best closeups of drakes. Hens settle down quickly after their arrival home and are almost tame by the time their young hatch. Drakes maintain more of their wariness and alertness, but the desire to stay with the hen usually overcomes any urge to avoid me, the photographer. When you see a classic drake photo in this book that seems too good to be true, thanks should go to the docile hen that's usually just outside the borders of the picture.

Within a week of the paired birds' arrival to their nesting grounds, the unpaired drake mallards arrive and

This hen (left) is performing an inciting movement. She is looking in the direction of an unwelcome, unpaired male and performing rapid jabbing movements with her bill. This by itself will not repel the bachelor male that is disturbing the female, but it stimulates her mate into chasing the unpaired male away. In the photo above, she has brought her mate to attention. He is vocalizing to a nearby unpaired male; should vocalizing be unsuccessful, he will leave his spot and chase the intruder away.

The start of a three-bird chase. An unpaired male has flown in from the left side of the picture and put the paired hen to flight. Her mate is still on the water beneath her, but he will shortly take flight. Thus, most three-bird chases have the hen in the lead, an unpaired drake nipping at her tail, and the hen's mate bringing up the rear.

During copulation, the female supports almost the entire weight of the male and almost submerges. He grasps the nape of her neck to help keep from rolling off, plus perhaps to keep her head above water.

After copulation, together the pair bathe and dry their wings before retiring to a secluded spot.

attempt to court any hens they come across. Such attempts at this stage are usually fruitless: The paired female typically performs an "inciting movement," turning her head sideways and jabbing her bill backwards along her flank or breast, which stimulates her mate to drive off the intruder. Another common occurrence is for the unpaired "bachelor" drake to approach the paired female from behind and force her to take flight. He will then follow close behind, with the paired male bringing up the rear. Such "three-bird flights" are a common sight among most species of waterfowl in the spring. The birds may fly anywhere from a few yards to several miles before the unpaired drake breaks off his pursuit and allows the mated pair to resume their courtship.

It is rare that a bachelor male successfully breaks up a mated pair of ducks. What I occasionally see is that an unpaired male is able to keep the paired drake away from his mate long enough for another unpaired male to mate with the female. Hormones are at work here, not thinking ability. My feeling is that the interference of an unpaired male might actually help keep the mated pair together: The drake's defense of the hen seems to help cement the pair bond for that season. But having bachelor males nearby isn't always just a nuisance. Should something happen to the paired drake, a few unpaired males close by helps to insure that the hen will find a new mate and lay fertile eggs.

Most of the courting has already taken place by the time mallards reach their nesting grounds. The drake has used his eye-catching green head and upturned tail to attract a mate, and any courting that now occurs is primarily to maintain their rather loose pair bond.

Once courting has been successful and the nesting area has been selected, mating occurs. Copulation takes place several times a day, on the water, with the hen almost completely submerged because she supports the weight of the male during mating. Prior to mating, both birds perform a vertical pumping movement with their

This drake is in the "head-up, tail-up" courting position. Such a pose displays his iridescent green head and curled undertail coverts to best advantage and will be helpful in attracting a mate.

heads, followed by the hen flattening herself on the water (the "soliciting position") as a sign that she is ready for mating. After mating, the drake swims around her before both retire to a nearby area to bathe and preen.

I tread easy during mating and the interaction that occurs just before mating, trying not to interrupt or disturb the ducks. I've photographed a few copulations, when I sensed I would not interfere with the pair, but by and large I keep my powder dry for another day. Sooner or later I'll get everything on film; in almost every case where I've not pushed a situation I've been rewarded later on with photos that might not have been possible otherwise. I remember one particularly touchy pair that I danced around throughout their courtship and mating. One quiet, sunny morning I sensed that a bit more trust had developed between me and the ducks, and I was able to get close enough to obtain perhaps my best picture of the pair at their loafing bar. When I look at the completely relaxed, regal drake with his mate full of eggs and tail feathers plucked to line her nest, I consider the photograph an example of what the birds have chosen to give to me, rather than what I've taken from them.

A pair of mallards at their loafing bar: a regal, relaxed drake and a hen with plucked tail feathers and rump swollen with eggs. Such a photo would not have resulted had I not used patience and restraint in the preceding weeks while following this pair. **Inset:** *Because mallards and all other water-fowl mate on the water, a penis, the corkscrew-shaped appendage, is necessary to insure that sperm are transferred into the female rather than lost in the water.*

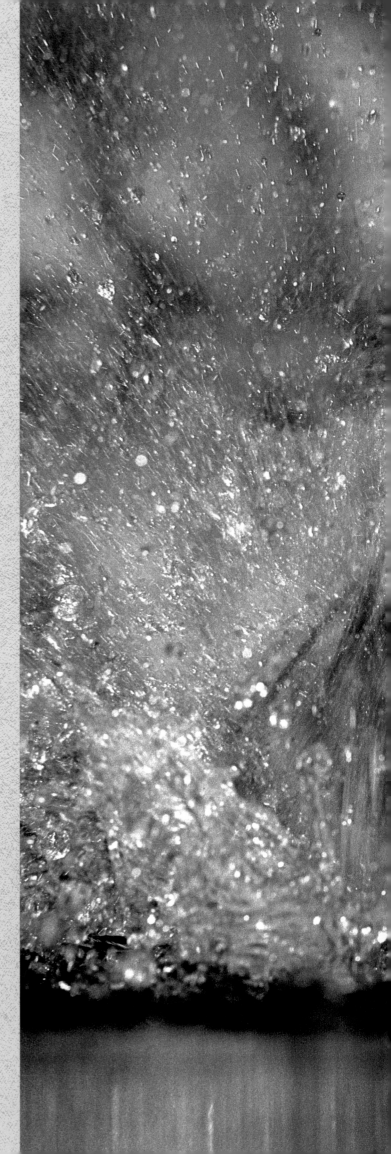

GOOD GROOMING

A mallard's feathers are important to it for flight, insulation, waterproofing, streamlining, and camouflage. Little surprise that they spend about an hour each morning and again in the afternoon keeping the feathers in perfect condition. Most ducks commonly do this after feeding and follow a fairly well-defined procedure, as shown with this hen mallard.

A good bath starts the preening and helps soak water into the water-repellent plumage. Wings need to be quickly dried after bathing, because they will be used to quickly leave an area should danger threaten, and waterlogged wings are not very functional. Because of this, bathing is almost always followed by a series of quick wing flaps, which sheds much of the water. Similarly, a mallard will shake its body from tail to head, removing excess water from the rest of the feathers. Once the droplets of water are removed, the hen uses her bill to work over feathers individually, pulling them through her bill in much the same way we comb our hair. She gives her wings priority, again because they are vital for her safety. A duck's flexible neck can reach nearly each body feather, but just like we cannot stick our elbows in our ears, the feathers at the base of the neck and on up are out of reach, and mallards will scratch the head feathers with a foot to help dry and arrange them. During preening, badly worn feathers are removed. Once everything is dry, the mallard will use its bill to collect and apply oil to the feathers to make them waterproof again. When completed, ducks typically find a quiet spot to rest and digest their meal.

After a bath, the mallard flaps its wings
and shakes its body to throw water off.

The dapper mallard carefully repositions
its feathers with its bill.

Once aged and tattered feathers are
removed, the mallard spreads waterproofing oil on its feathers with its bill.

This hen has taken feathers from her breast to line the nest. In so doing, she has exposed a bare area of skin that, when put in contact with the eggs during incubation, will help keep them warm. Ornithologists call such an area a "brood patch."

THE CYCLE
BEGINS

Just as the hen chooses a mate and sets the agenda for courting and mating, she alone chooses and prepares a nest site. An area adjacent to water in tall grasses is preferred, but mallards will nest up to a quarter mile from water when breeding densities—numbers of nesting pairs—are high, and they will readily take to appropriately sized nest boxes placed on the ground. Adequate concealment is probably the biggest factor in the hen's choosing of a nest site. The hen will commonly make her choice within a week after arriving in the area, flying in the evening from her waiting point to explore the surrounding area for suitable nest locations.

Throughout most of their range, mallards start nesting during the last three weeks of April. If they nest much later, their young won't be on the wing before the droughts of August; any earlier and they run the risk of bad weather causing nest failure. I remember one particularly eager hen who had her clutch half completed before the ice left the lake near my home. The lake's sudden melting, plus lots of rain, raised water levels so high that the hen had to use her bill to push the eggs to a new nest location on higher ground a few yards farther away from the shoreline. Not all mallards are as enterprising, and sudden cold snaps or heavy rains and hailstorms take their toll of nests.

A mallard nest is not an elaborate affair. The hen will wriggle her breast into the damp ground or grasses to form a depression only one or two inches deep. She begins to lay eggs within a day or two of making a nest bowl, depositing an egg a day, usually in the morning. Eight to twelve eggs make up a normal clutch, and she adds a few bits of adjacent vegetation with each egg. The female also plucks feathers and down, mainly from her breast, to line the nest and cover the eggs. These feathers are likely to have been loosened

by a partial molting process that occurs at the start of nesting.

It is during this two-week period of nest-site selection and egg laying that the mallard hen and drake begin to go their separate ways. The drake stays in the area, but he usually does not accompany the hen to the nest site because his brilliant coloring could attract predators such as egg-eating skunks and raccoons. He instead will fly with the hen from her waiting point and circle back to this spot while she tends the nest.

Mallard nests are simple and usually within one hundred feet of the water's edge, and occasionally mallards will nest on top of muskrat houses (above).

This hen, who has been laying her eggs, has joined her mate at his loafing bar. While he stands guard, she can feed, bathe, preen (as in this photo), and rest in peace, conserving energy for the rigors of incubation.

INCUBATION

Because all ducklings must hatch at about the same time in order to leave the nest together, the hen does not begin incubation until her clutch is nearly complete. After depositing her first eggs, she will instead return to her drake, often at the waiting site. Such a spot now becomes a "loafing bar," an area the drake keeps clear of other males in order to allow his egg-laying mate time to feed, bathe, preen, rest, and mate in peace. Most of her energies must be directed toward egg production, not for fending off attacks of intruding males.

Once her clutch is complete and incubation begins, the hen will leave the nest only in the morning and evening for an hour or two, leaving a heavy layer of down over the eggs to minimize their cooling. It is during this first few days of incubation that many pair bonds are broken. Without a hen in his constant company, the drake gradually abandons the loafing bar that he has been protecting, and instead may group together with other deserted males. This is a fascinating process to watch. Whereas only a day or two earlier, an unpaired drake's approach to a mallard pair would elicit an immediate rebuff from the paired drake; now the two drakes chatter to each other and may go off together, leaving the hen to herself. Should the unpaired male force the paired hen into flight, as mentioned above, at this stage the trio might fly in tandem for a while only to have the two males fly off together.

Should an unpaired female who hasn't yet nested be in the area, she will be pursued and forcibly mated by these newly deserted males. While such rape flights distress the hens earlier in the nest cycle, my impression is that an unpaired hen or a hen who has lost her first clutch in some ways does not discourage this behavior in the males. Any attempts to flee the males are halfhearted, circling flights where the males are sure to catch her. A hen with

Incubating hens leave the nest once or twice a day to feed, bathe, and preen. Groups of drakes are still in the area, but successfully nesting hens seek out very quiet areas when away from the nest to avoid the males.

Occasional three-bird chases still take place this late in the cycle, but frequently they will result in the two drakes flying off together, leaving the hen to her incubation duties.

As incubation proceeds, pair bonds are gradually broken, and drakes leave nesting areas to join other drakes in more isolated molting spots. Here, they will complete their body molt, then shed their flight feathers. Only in August, when new flight feathers have grown in, will they rejoin the now-grown broods they fathered.

Occasionally, I will see an encounter between a behind-schedule drake and an early-hatching brood of ducks. In rare cases, an uneasy truce is reached, and a hen may allow occasional contact of her brood with a drake. Drakes are usually quite aggressive toward the ducklings (inset).

a nest of eggs is only away from them and exposed to the drakes for an hour or so a day, while the unpaired hens are almost always on the water or in the air, exposed to the attentions of the drakes.

Drakes will stay in breeding condition until early June, when loss of their distinctively curled black undertail coverts and first disappearance of green feathers around the eyes signals the end of their roles in this season's nesting. They will continue to flock together and will typically leave the nesting area in June for more isolated molting locations. From here on out, the responsibility for the future generation rests completely with the hens.

On completion of her clutch, the hen plucks down to form a heavy insulating ring around her and begins incubation. Incubation averages four weeks, but may vary a few days either way, depending on the weather and attentiveness of the female. Cold weather or the hen abandoning the nest for more than an hour or two each day will slow the embryos' development. Warm conditions or a particularly attentive hen will speed things up a bit.

Besides skunks and raccoons, other predators such as foxes and magpies prey on eggs. By picking a well-camouflaged nest site and not locating near other hens' nest sites, the hens make it difficult for predators to find all the nests in a particular area. Although the hen leaves her incubation duties once or twice a day to feed, bathe, and preen, she further complicates things for predators by hiding the eggs with a cover of down before leaving; this also keeps the eggs from cooling too much before she returns. A hen will also take a circuitous route when returning to her nest on the chance that a predator is following her. I've seen hens take as much as ten minutes to cover the last few yards to their nests, zigzagging and pausing at times to check for any nearby movement or danger. Only when she is satisfied that she has been undetected will "Mom" return to the nest, shove

From the time of egg laying through fledging, young mallards face an array of predators both on land and on the water. The stealthy great blue heron occasionally takes a duckling from above the water (note the out-of-focus mallard in the foreground).

A destroyed nest, probably the result of a raid by a fox, skunk, or raccoon. This is one reason I steer clear of photographing nests: Even if I do not disturb the hen, the scent I leave could give the nest location away. Any located nest will likely become a destroyed nest because the hen usually is unable to successfully defend it against an aggressive predator.

Left: This hen is returning to her nest. She occasionally pokes her head above the grasses to check for danger. I never fail to marvel at the stealth hens use to avoid giving away nest locations; even when I know where the nest is, the hen will routinely fool me as I watch her return to the eggs.

In the northern limits of the mallard's range, arctic foxes raid any nest they locate, and will feed on the eggs or on ducklings they manage to catch. Once the eggs have hatched, snapping turtles take their share of ducklings from below the water surface.

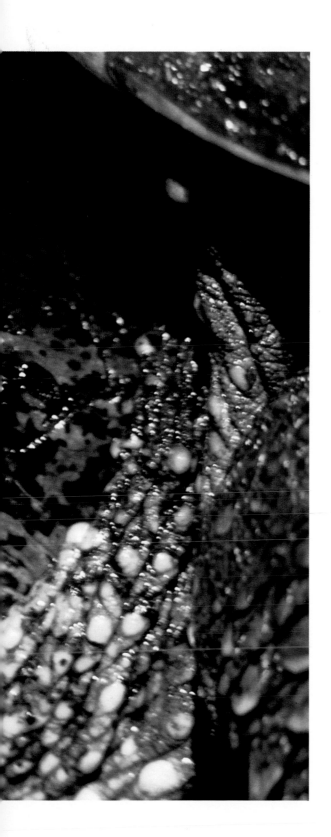

the down covering aside, and resume incubation.

As during mating, this is one time I try to give the mallards their distance. While the hen is adept at not attracting the attention of predators, my presence nearby and even the scent I leave could lure a raccoon, fox, or skunk. I generally prefer to lay my camera down and watch from a distance, marveling at the stealth she uses. Perhaps the twenty-eight-day incubation period is a test for motherhood. The hen will have to shepherd her young through their first ten weeks of life, and the incubation period is a good test of her abilities. As I said in the introduction, photography involves a lot more than taking pictures. The hours I spend in a blind *not* taking photos, but rather thinking about what nature has shown me and trying to make some sense or logic of it all, are as enjoyable as the relatively short periods of time I'm actually working with a camera.

The hen will commonly return to the same area to feed that she used prior to completion of egg laying. Drakes are often still in the area and will attempt to mate with any hen they locate. While this is advantageous for a hen that has lost her clutch and attempts to renest, courting males are an inconvenience for the incubating hens, and they typically greet drakes not with the soliciting posture of acceptance but rather with the head back, tail up, mouth agape "gesture of repulsion" posture. The aggressive drakes will still pursue her, but not to the point of exhaustion as they do with unmated hens. The brooding female must instead conserve her energy for incubation and any defense of the nest that becomes necessary.

The superb camouflage of the hen and the concealed nest site she chooses is her best defense against predators. As long as she feels she has not been detected, she will hold tight on the nest, regardless of how close a predator approaches. Once she thinks she has been seen, however, she will become quite animated in defense of the nest. If the predator is still some distance away, she may move

Should an incubating hen encounter a drake on her short trips off the nest, she has a posture and voice that will discourage him. This gesture of repulsion display consists of her lifting her wings while throwing her head back and giving a very abrasive call.

By the end of June, hens that were unsuccessful in nesting stop attempting to renest and instead flock together much like the males did a month earlier. The hens in this picture have attempted nesting two or even three times. They've now simply run out of time, because any nesting begun in July would not result in young until August, and fledging would not occur until fall. Any late summer drought would likely doom the brood, and inexperienced young would have many more difficulties during migration.

FIRST WEEKS

As hatching time nears, the hen feels the ducklings move inside the eggs, and she in turn utters a low clucking call to the young. This is believed to stimulate the young, who use their bills and the hardened egg tooth at their bills' tip to slowly chip themselves out of the egg.

Hatching takes a good day, and the young become quite exhausted from breaking out of their shells. Under the warmth of the mother, the ducklings' down dries off, and they rest up in preparation for leaving the nest. Hens continue to cluck during this time; each hen has a distinctive voice and the young quickly learn to recognize their mother's unique sound. It will become important when the hen escorts her brood through dense vegetation and must use her voice to keep everyone together. The young are said to "imprint" on their mother's call, and because of her movement they become imprinted on her visually, recognizing themselves as mallards in the process.

A full eight weeks will pass before the ducklings take wing. During this time, they will increase their weight by a factor of thirty and will develop many of the skills necessary for becoming independent.

Ducklings dry off and leave the nest within a day of hatching. The hen leads them directly to the nearest water for feeding, a distance ranging from a few feet to as much as a mile. Insects are almost the exclusive diet of ducklings during their first week of life, when they require a diet especially high in protein. Because most mallard nesting starts during the last three weeks of April, and incubation lasts for four weeks, the majority of hatchings occurs within a week or two of Memorial Day, an ideal time for ducklings as this is when major hatches of insects also occur and food supplies are abundant. The hen's only role in feeding is to lead her brood to appropriate food sources,

Imprinting in mallards is both vocal and visual. Each hen has her own unique clucking that the ducklings learn early in life, perhaps in the day or two before they hatch. Similarly, the hen bonds to the cheeping her ducklings make (above right) and can recognize their collective call while not responding to the similar calls of other broods.

A hen leads her week-old ducklings to an appropriate feeding area. Ducklings visually imprint on the first moving thing they see. In almost all cases, this is their mother, whom they will obediently follow.

generally shallow, warm water places where insects hatch. Vegetation is first breaking through the water surface at this time, providing concealment for the ducklings as they go about plucking resting insects from plant stems and skimming them from the water surface. I remember many cold, rainy Memorial Day weekends of my youth when the lake at first seemed lifeless, only to have a hen mallard and newly hatched brood quickly skitter by, hugging the cover of the shoreline.

The dark yellow "natal down" ducklings are born with is noticeable for their first two weeks of life. The natal down is surprisingly good camouflage. Its color, plus the ducklings' small size, makes the ducklings resemble the yellow pond lily, a commonly occurring plant in mallard habitat. More than once I've roused myself from daydreaming in my blind and reflexively snapped a picture of a pond lily, thinking it was a nearby duckling. I'm sure I'm not the only carnivore so fooled. A bald eagle or heron may occasionally snatch a duckling from above, but the youngsters' main danger at this early stage comes from predators beneath the water, primarily the snapping turtle and pike. By sticking to shallow water, the ducklings can minimize the chances of these predators coming up from beneath them, but mallards also use deeper, open water in going from one feeding location to another, and it is common for a brood of ten ducklings to be down to seven or eight after a few weeks.

The hen's role in defense of her young is primarily one of prevention. While the young feed almost constantly during daylight, the hen is just as constantly on the alert for danger, and by moving and calling she will lead the ducklings away from potential danger and problems when possible. If danger threatens, she will often perform a distraction display, quickly moving away from the brood and splashing along the water surface to create as much eye-catching movement and ear-catching noise as possible to divert the predator's attention. I have seen

When ducklings hatch, they are clad in a dark yellow natal down (above). As the bird grows, lighter colored juvenile down emerges amongst the natal down (below).

Ducklings feed primarily on protein-rich insects during their first few weeks of life. The first broods hatch in late May, right when a large hatch of insects takes place. This hen is feeding with her young on a concentration of insects, seen as a white coloring on the water surface.

The camouflage of ducklings is surprisingly good. While they may seem brightly colored when seen in closeup, from a distance they resemble and can be confused with the yellow pond lilies they commonly swim among.

Should danger approach, the hen quickly distances herself from the young and pretends to be wounded. By flailing her wings and creating a ruckus, she draws the predator's attention away from the young, who huddle quietly and un-noticeably nearby (above). Once she has lured the predator away, she flies back to her brood and calls them to her side from their hiding place (inset).

Above: *For several hours in the middle of the day, ducklings nap, clustering together and soaking up the sun to retain heat while the mother keeps a constant vigil against predators.* **Inset:** *This brood of at least nineteen young is almost certainly the result of two broods merging after one mother died or was otherwise separated from her young. The adopting hen can be seen in the center of the group.*

hens rise from the water and splash down as if to indicate a broken wing or other inability to fly; such apparent vulnerability is a strong attraction for a predator, who quickly forgets the ducklings huddled safely nearby.

If a hen becomes separated from her brood during such times, her clucking or low quacking quickly brings the ducklings to her side once the danger is past. Similarly, should a duckling become separated from the pack, its "cheeping" sound will elicit the mother's quacking response and reunite the family. There are occasions when the hen is killed or becomes permanently separated from all or part of her brood, and in these cases the orphans will often merge with another family. The success of this varies, but most of the time the young are accepted, although I've seen some situations where the orphaned young stay together within the family and are never completely accepted by their cousins. I've counted as many as twenty-three ducklings in a merged brood. Any group of over fourteen or fifteen ducklings with one hen is probably two or more merged broods.

Although the hen does some snacking in between her guarding of the brood, her main meal usually occurs at midmorning. On sunny, warm days, I've often seen hens lead their young to a quiet, secluded place after a morning of feeding and then quickly fly away from them to feed, bathe, and preen in privacy. The young huddle together for warmth and take a nap during this ten-minute to half-hour period. Perhaps it is good that the hen leaves her young during this time, as her movements during bathing, preening, and feeding would call attention to the young. Although napping, at almost all times at least one duckling has its eyes open on the lookout for any movement. Such movement or sound quickly brings the duckling and its nestmates to attention. When the hen returns from her break, she will quack when nearing her brood, eliciting a peeping call from them in recognition of her voice and thereby allowing her to locate them.

Young ducklings (these are four days old) huddle together to help conserve heat while their mother is taking a short break to bathe and preen (above). Such eye-catching activity is best done away from the ducklings in order to not call attention to the young.

I've yet to figure out how the ducklings know when to follow their mother and when to seek cover. Somehow there's a communication beyond the human visual and auditory level that makes the ducklings bunch together when she leaves to fend off intruders or to do her midmorning preening. Yet when their mother is just moving quickly through the water, the ducklings speed up and stay near her. People who know I've been photographing the mallard for fifteen years wonder why I keep going back. "There's only so many photos you can take of these birds without it getting repetitious," they say; yet I cannot think of a single minute I've spent with the mallard that's been even similar to any other minute. I find something new in every moment, and for every behavior I begin to even slightly comprehend, several new questions arise.

Aside from guarding against danger, the hen also plays a vital role in protecting the young against cold and rain. The ducklings' down is quite waterproof, and their dark backsides help absorb the warmth of the sun, but most evenings the hen will brood her young for extra warmth. Occasionally, she will return with them to the original nest site to brood, but most any dry, concealed place near the water will suffice. The rapidly growing young take up more and more room under the hen, and she will commonly spread her wings to accommodate everyone. This same strategy works well during rainstorms, when her waterproof wings shield the young from most of the moisture and keep them from getting chilled. From a distance, such hens take on the appearance of turtles, because they keep their heads low and the outspread wings resemble a shell.

As the ducklings grow, it gets more and more difficult for everyone to fit under "Mom" for brooding. She compensates by partially spreading and cupping her wings, as this hen is doing. I especially see this during rainstorms, where the water-repellent wings become an umbrella for the young.

Preening movements are instinctive, not learned. Here a five-week-old juvenile mallard preens his breast in exactly the same manner as an adult would.

PATCHWORK DUCKLINGS

Mallard ducklings' early growth consists primarily of their bodies lengthening. At about two weeks of age, the lighter-colored "juvenile down" grows in among the natal down, so that the young always have a full down layer. This juvenile down becomes quite noticeable at three to four weeks of age for two reasons: The natal down fades in color, and, because the duckling's body has been growing, proportionately more of the duck is covered by juvenile down. Also at this age, the first juvenile feathers sprout along the young duck's sides, tail, and back, replacing the natal down. These first feathers are much better at insulating and protecting the duckling than its down was, and once these juvenile feathers have fully grown in (at six weeks of age), the hen will no longer have to brood the ducklings, even in the coolest weather.

Although the ducklings continue to forage for food, preen, and bathe as a group, they start to keep a bit of distance from each other because they no longer have to rely on each other's body heat for warmth. Their bodies are quite large now, and therefore a large amount of heat is generated and conserved in relation to when they were in the downy stage of life.

In mid-June the ducklings are four weeks of age, and have taken on many of their mother's behaviors. They "tip up" to feed, they bathe, and they preen as if they were full-grown mallards. Such preening movements must be instinctive, because individual ducklings raised without contact with other birds perform the same movements. I have to laugh every time I see a young duckling going through extensive preening gestures in the area of a wing that is not yet there. Such movements might seem superfluous now, but in a few weeks they will be very important to the wing's maintenance. Wings are the last appendage to develop, and even at five weeks of age they lag far behind the

By three weeks of age, the ducklings' bodies have greatly lengthened and a full coat of juvenile down has grown in among the darker yellow natal down. These two ducklings still keep huddled together to conserve heat.

Once an insulating layer of feathers emerges, a duckling can maintain its body temperature without its mother's brooding or huddling with its nestmates. These two-week-old ducklings still keep close together in part for warmth (top), but by five weeks of age (above), they feel comfortable keeping a bit of distance between each other.

rest of the bird's growth. This four- to five-week age is commonly referred to as the "ugly duckling" stage of growth. Patches of worn, faded down are still present, contrasting the rich juvenile feathering that is emerging; the feet and bill are large and adultlike, but the stubby wings look hopelessly small and unlikely to ever lift the comparatively large body they are connected to.

By six weeks of age, the young mallard is almost fully grown. Slowing of growth in other areas allows the channelling of surplus nutrients to the wings, and in only two more weeks the duck will be capable of flight. The young mallards repeatedly flap and exercise the growing wings, strengthening the pectoral muscles that will eventually power their flight.

At four weeks of age, the first feathers of the juvenile plumage emerge along the back near where the wings attach. This juvenile mallard displays a hodgepodge of natal down, juvenile down, and juvenile feathering, the so-called "ugly duckling" stage of development. Its wings seem hopelessly behind schedule in development when compared to the rapidly growing body.

At six weeks of age (inset), the duckling's body is almost full size, and energy for growth is channelled to the wings. Blood can be seen (blue color) in the shafts of this duckling's flight feathers. This is how nutrients are transported to the developing feathers. Once completely grown, the blood supply is shut off, and the feathers can firmly attach to the bones of the wing. Even though this final stage of wing development is several weeks away, this bird is exercising its breast muscles to strengthen them for future flights.

A PARADE OF PLUMAGES

Most of us recognize the distinctive adult plumages of the male and female mallards, but these ducks go through three successive layers of down and feathers before acquiring their adult dress.

During their first few weeks of life, mallard ducklings wear dark yellow coats of natal down. As their bodies lengthen and heads grow, lighter yellow juvenile down grows in among the natal down. Feathers sprout at four weeks of age, and a month later these first feathers are almost completely grown in. This rich brown juvenile plumage, as shown by these two males, will be present only in the summer of their first year of life. By September, the piecework juveniles molt into their recognizable adult plumage.

Adult feathers must be replaced each year due to wear or damage. The adults molt their feathers in the summer, after breeding and nesting, and the molting process is most noticeable in the male. This drake is well into his summer or "eclipse" plumage. Note that the feathers on his wings are still intact; they won't be molted until he has a camouflaged, henlike body coloring. Once that is attained, in July, he will shed his flight feathers; the loss grounds him for the month while his new flight feathers grow in. Once able to fly, the brown body feathering is replaced by a new breeding coat, and the drake is ready for his fall migration. Hen mallards follow the same cycle, although their eclipse plumage is much the same as their breeding plumage. Thus,

Two male juveniles.

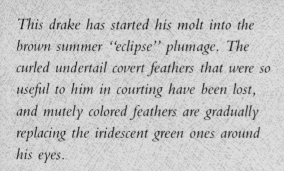

This drake has started his molt into the brown summer "eclipse" plumage. The curled undertail covert feathers that were so useful to him in courting have been lost, and mutely colored feathers are gradually replacing the iridescent green ones around his eyes.

during each molting cycle, the ducks replace their wing feathers once and body feathers twice.

Occasionally, for genetic or hormonal reasons, an unusually large or small amount of pigment is deposited in the feathers as they grow. Large amounts of pigment result in a melanistic (dark) bird. Birds like this nesting hen are still well camouflaged and are not at a particularly increased risk of predation because of their different color. When little or no pigment is in the feathers, the bird is termed leucystic. The resulting white color is much more noticeable to predators, and such a bird is often quickly culled from the populations. I photographed this leucystic hen in the company of normally colored mallards. In addition to her leucysism, the flight feathers did not grow completely, and she had to run along the water to take flight much like a diving duck. Note that her eyes, bill, and feet are a normal color. If pigment were also missing from those areas, she would be considered an albino, something quite rare among wild ducks.

A leucystic mallard.

A melanistic mallard.

These eight juveniles are eight weeks old and ready for their first awkward flight. Their mother (fourth from right) is well into her summer molt, and close examination shows that her folded flight feathers are missing, while well grown in on her offspring. Once the hen's flight feathers are regrown, she will join her brood in flight, well before it is necessary to migrate.

FIRST FLIGHT

Once the young no longer require their mother for brooding, at five or six weeks of age, she will begin her annual feather molt, shedding all her flight feathers at once and growing a new plumage in about a month's time. She will then be on the wing in time to accompany her young on their first flights. There are also cases where the hen will delay her molt until the young reach flight stage and then desert them to molt in privacy.

Mallards commonly take their first flight at around eight weeks of age, generally during the month of July. In the Arctic, however, they can be on the wing in as little as six weeks. Biologists believe that in the Arctic, the cooler temperatures stimulate production of thyroxin (a growth hormone), and the north's long hours of sunlight during the summer increase the rate of feather growth. The longer span of daylight also allows for continual feeding.

In contrast to the instinctive behaviors of bathing, preening, and feeding, the fine points of flight are mainly learned behaviors, and considerable practice is necessary to perfect them. The first flight is preceded by several weeks of wing-flapping to strengthen the pectoral muscles. Takeoffs and landings are especially clumsy when the first flights are attempted in July. I've often seen juvenile ducklings run along the water for several dozen yards, in loonlike fashion, only to crash back onto the water's surface when they run out of gas. Occasionally one of the stronger birds is able to take to the air, which elicits a raucous quacking from its brothers and sisters. Within a few days the family is able to circle the lake as a group, and the newly fledged birds bump into each other occasionally as they learn to handle the gusts of wind and other variables they will encounter every day from here on out.

As flight stage nears, families become more tolerant of each other. Before

Up until the ducklings fledge, broods keep their distance from each other. Should two mothers encounter each other, a shoving match and fight almost inevitably result.

this, mothers of young would shove and fight each other any time they came in contact. In contrast, families now begin to socialize, and flights of a half dozen birds now turn into flights of dozens as the days noticeably shorten, the nesting season ends, and the mallards prepare for autumn.

Mallards reach sexual maturity in their first autumn of life. A sign of their approaching maturity is the distinguishing color of their bills. Ducklings appear virtually identical until around six weeks of age, when their dark brown bills begin to change to an orange color for females or green for males. **Left:** Once the young have fledged, usually in July, families tolerate each other and gradually merge in anticipation for the fall flight south.

In some years, mallards remain in northern Wisconsin long into fall. But by mid-October, most nesting mallards have left to congregate with birds from nearby areas. This photo was taken at Crex Meadows Wildlife Area, sixty miles south of my home, and there could well be a few of my mallards among the hundreds in the photograph. **Inset:** *This drake was photographed in front of my northern Wisconsin house in early December, an unusually late date. In spite of subzero temperatures, he stayed nearby for several weeks longer. Note that he has recovered his full breeding plumage.*

A certain tension seems to develop as flocks build up during the fall. Finally, the restless energy forces part of the flock to break off and scatter southward.

Future Cycles

Large wintering flocks of mallards no longer darken the skies, but several hundred in a group are still one of nature's most impressive sights. With a little help from us, sights like this will be around for centuries to come.

Future Cycles

Much has been written recently about the decline in duck numbers throughout North America, and the mallard has not escaped from this decline. The highest accurately recorded breeding population of mallards occurred in 1958, with an estimated thirteen million spring adults. Less than half this number returned to nest in 1989. On a thirty-year average, total breeding populations of North America's ducks in general and the mallard in particular have dropped 25 percent.

A certain amount of this is normal. Duck populations run in cycles: Large numbers of birds are produced in wet years, and relatively little successful nesting occurs during droughts. Millions of years of evolution have adapted the mallard's behavior to deal with these natural variations. On average, roughly half of all mallard nests hatch young, half of all mallard young that hatch survive to fledging, and half of these young ducks in turn make it through the winter to nest the next spring. This averages out to one or two young surviving to adulthood for each nesting attempt, which, over a one- or two-year typical adult nesting life, is sufficient to replace the parents in the breeding population and keep mallard numbers self-perpetuating.

What currently complicates things for mallards and other ducks is the addition of other factors, mostly manmade, to which mallards have trouble adapting quickly enough. One problem at a time may be tolerable, but many problems piled on top of drought conditions have created difficulties.

All life needs suitable habitat: food, water, breathing room, and a place to raise a family. In a large sense, every problem ducks face directly or indirectly affects their habitat. Every time a pond dries up, either from drought or intentional drainage, there are that many fewer options for ducks to choose from when nesting. The mallard is more adaptable than most waterfowl, able to nest some distance from water. But it may have to compromise by selecting a nest site with less concealment than a pondside location offers, and this in turn makes the eggs more likely to be lost to predators. It has recently come to light that foxes, which have in some ways benefitted from our agricultural practices, take large numbers of eggs from prairie field nests each year. Losses of up to 70 percent have been recorded from predation by foxes, raccoons, skunks, and other predators in certain study areas. A field may seem a desirable place to nest at first, but if it is mowed before hatching time, the eggs will almost inevitably be destroyed, or the hen will desert her nest because of disturbances and the lack of cover.

Water is important not only for raising young, but also as a source of nutrients. Contaminated water can pose long-term problems for ducks. In the Central Valley of California, for instance, irrigation water has been used to flood waterfowl wintering and resting areas. The heavy metals and other pesticide residues the water contains are taken up by the ducks, and this in turn results in birth defects and increased susceptibility to other diseases. In low-water years, this is complicated by the larger and larger number of mallards and other ducks concentrating at what few water areas remain. Ducks are gregarious by nature, but this is a two-edged sword. There is increased safety in numbers, but too much crowding stresses the birds, and consequently lowers their resistance to disease. Outbreaks of cholera, botulism, and other contagious diseases occur annually among flocks of waterfowl. Because weakened or diseased ducks will by instinct seek out isolated areas to attempt to recuperate, their deaths may not be noticed, and it is therefore difficult to know how much of an effect disease brought about by overcrowding has on reducing waterfowl populations.

Much the same can be said for the lead-containing

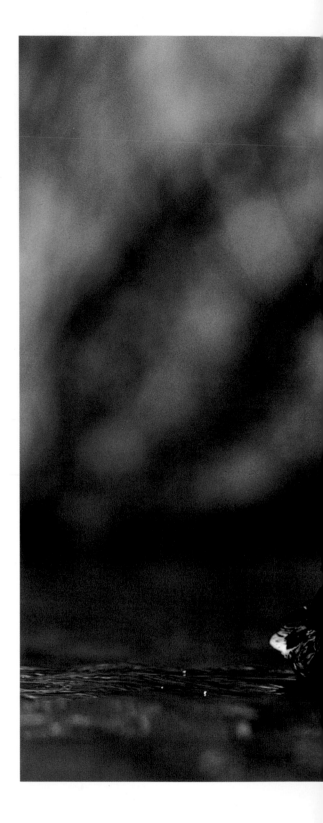

Although the mallard adapts well to encroaching urban environments, a clean, suitable habitat with plenty of water, in both winter and summer, is vital if the mallard is to survive. These mallards are sharing this narrows with goldeneyes and ringnecks.

shot that persists in the bottoms of many ponds, lakes, and rivers. Waterfowl consume these pellets during their feeding, and, when lodged in the bird's gizzard, the pellets are ground and some lead is released into the bloodstream, causing damage to the liver and kidneys as well as impairing digestion. The resulting poor diet further weakens the bird. As few as one or two #6 lead shot pellets are enough to kill an adult mallard, and as many as seventy-six pellets have been counted in a mallard's gizzard. When found, lead-poisoned ducks have typically lost half their body weight from impaired digestion.

It is estimated that up to 4 percent of the mallards along the Mississippi Flyway die each year from consuming lead shot. Even though nontoxic steel shot has replaced lead in most hunting areas, about ten million pounds of lead shot was annually deposited beneath North American waters, starting with the market gunners a century ago. This lead remains for a long time, and while much of it is in deep water out of the reach of ducks, drought conditions have lowered water levels in some areas enough that ducks, geese, and especially the long-necked swans pick up pellets that previously were unobtainable.

Waterfowl hunting has been regulated since World War I, and quotas are now indexed to such factors as the number of birds of each species produced each year. In addition, many hunters now practice voluntary restraint, taking fewer birds than they are allowed or hunting only the drakes. In most duck populations, there is a surplus of males, probably to insure that hens who lose their first nest in the spring successfully remate, and possibly to stimulate competition in winter courtship. The sex balance in mallards is relatively close, with about fifty-two drakes in a population of one hundred birds. But the aggressive, polygamous nature of the mallard drake helps insure successful mating with all spring hens. Within certain boundaries, the number of mallard hens (not the number of drakes) is the determinant for how much nesting occurs.

When concern was first raised over duck populations, most of the attention was rightly placed on restoring and preserving nesting habitat. Further studies have shown that wintering habitat also has a big effect on spring nesting success. The fat reserves the hen builds up over winter affect her nesting and the number of eggs laid the coming spring. The mallard's ability to use waste grain in fields during winter has been an advantage here, but more efficient harvesting methods and plowing the stubble under in the fall has reduced the waste grain available to them. Many farmers have now switched to a "no till" type of agriculture, where stubble is left standing and serves as an important food source for ducks and many other species of wildlife.

The problems facing our mallard and other ducks are complicated, varied, and yet very much interconnected. Drought or drainage reduces nest numbers and concentrates the birds. This connection stresses them, further exposing them to predation and disease. But the mallard is a tough, resilient species, still existing in sufficiently large numbers to be able to bounce back if given half a chance.

I think back to the first cold, windy days of spring, when the old hens return to stand in the icy slush and quack out their joy at returning home. I think of the warm, sunny days of late May, when they cautiously lead a new generation of young from the nest. I think of the frosty, foggy mornings of autumn when previously aloof families come together in harmony. I think of the bitter cold, snowy winter mornings when the click of my camera shutter is drowned out by the thunder of hundreds of mallard wings beating against the air. For these and countless other experiences, I believe the mallard deserves every chance we can give it.

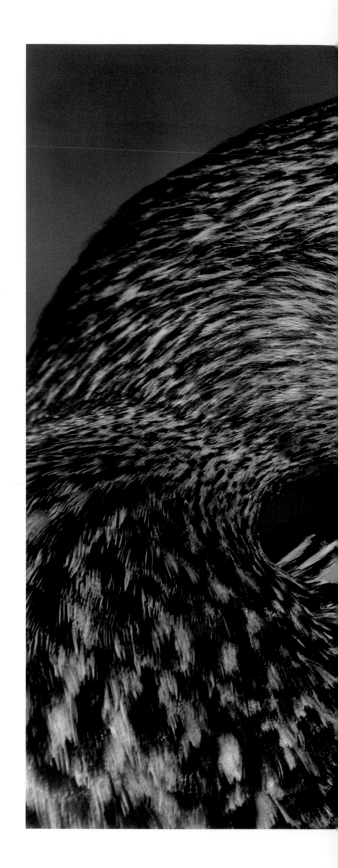

ORGANIZATIONS

The effort—sometimes battle—to conserve and restore wilderness and its inhabitants continues. Mallards, like other wild creatures, depend somewhat upon human awareness and action: It is up to us to reserve unspoiled wetlands and cleanse polluted habitat for the mallard to endure. Several organizations benefit the mallard and other wild animals and their habitats. Below are a few of the organizations and their self-descriptions; write to them to see how you can help.

Canadian Wildlife Federation
1673 Carling Avenue
Ottawa, Ontario K2A 3Z1

The Canadian Wildlife Federation's goals are to foster understanding of natural processes so that people may live in harmony with the land and its resources for the long-term benefit and enrichment of society; to maintain a substantial program of information and education based on ecological principles; and to conduct or sponsor research and scientific investigation.

The Canadian Wildlife Federation's description is from page 247 of the *1990 Conservation Directory,* published by the National Wildlife Federation.

Ducks Unlimited
One Waterfowl Way
Long Grove, IL 60047

Ducks Unlimited
1190 Waverly Street
Winnipeg, Manitoba, R3T 2E2

Ducks Unlimited, Inc., is a private, nonprofit membership organization dedicated to conserving wetland habitat for waterfowl and other wildlife. Its mission: To increase and perpetuate North American waterfowl by protecting, enhancing, restoring, and managing wetland systems and associated uplands critical to their annual cycle. Since its inception in 1937, Ducks Unlimited has raised over $650 million to conserve more than 5.5 million acres of valuable habitat throughout Canada, the United States, and Mexico. Over 600 wildlife species now look to DU-enhanced acreage for their habitat needs.

North American Wildlife Foundation
102 Wilmont Road, Suite 410
Deerfield, IL 60015

The North American Wildlife Foundation is dedicated to reversing the decline in North America's waterfowl populations. Since 1938, it has been the sponsor of the Delta Waterfowl and Wetlands Research Station and more recently has launched the Prairie Farming Program, Adopt A Pothole Program, Wild Duck Rearing and Release Program, Delta Station Press, and Voluntary Restraint Program. All these efforts draw on Delta's research experience in an effort to demonstrate actual activities which can benefit waterfowl and wetlands and to communicate the results to waterfowlers and conservationists. All contributors to NAWF receive the *Waterfowl Report,* a quarterly newsletter.

National Wildlife Federation
1400 Sixteenth Street Northwest
Washington, D.C. 20036

The National Wildlife Federation, organized in 1936, is a nonprofit conservation education organization dedicated to creating and encouraging an awareness among the people of the world of the need for wise use and proper management of those resources of the earth upon which our lives and welfare depend: soil, air, water, forests, minerals, plant life, and wildlife. The National Wildlife Federation undertakes a comprehensive conservation education program, distributes numerous periodicals and educational materials, sponsors outdoor education programs in conservation, and litigates environmental disputes in an effort to conserve natural resources and wildlife.

North American Waterfowl Plan
North American Waterfowl and Wetlands Office
340 Arlington Square
1849 "C" Street Northwest
Washington, D.C. 20240

North American Waterfowl Management Implementation
Canadian Wildlife Service
17th Floor, Place Vincent Massey
351 Boulevard St. Joseph
Hull, Quebec K1A OH3

The North American Waterfowl Management Plan is a fifteen-year program to help restore wetlands and migratory bird populations in the United States, Canada, and Mexico. Partners in the effort are the federal governments of the three countries, fifty states, and twelve provinces and territories, and more than two hundred conservation groups. The North American Waterfowl and Wetlands Office coordinates U.S. activities of the plan under the U.S. Department of the Interior's Fish and Wildlife Service. Canadian coordination of the plan is done by the North American Waterfowl Management Implementation.

Wildlife Management Institute
Suite 725, 1101 Fourteenth Street Northwest
Washington, D.C. 20005

The Wildlife Management Institute is a nonprofit, scientific, and educational organization dedicated to the improved management of wildlife and related natural resources. Founded in 1911, WMI is based in Washington, D.C. Its small staff of experienced natural resource educated and trained professionals works on request with state and federal officials, Congress, the White House, conservation organization administrators, university educators, and other resource professionals to develop, implement, advance, and monitor scientific programs to restore, enhance, and perpetuate wildlife populations and their habitats. WMI is actively involved in such programs and activities as the North American Waterfowl Management Plan, the Cooperative Wildlife Research Unit Program, Farm Act conservation provisions, appropriations for federal lands and resource management agencies, the annual North American Wildlife and Natural Resources Conference, and others.

Index

About the Author

Scott Nielsen is an avian taxidermist and photographer specializing in waterfowl and birds of prey. He holds degrees and advanced training from the University of Wisconsin, University of Arizona, and Northwestern University. While at Northwestern, he studied under Leon Pray at the Field Museum of Natural History and was able to prepare many of the world's rarest birds, including remounting specimens of the now extinct Labrador duck and passenger pigeon.

Since 1968, his studio has been located near the historic portage between the St. Croix and Brule rivers in northwestern Wisconsin. Although much of his photography is done in far-reaching places, most is taken within a few miles of his isolated home. Two pairs of bald eagles and dozens of songbird species nest within walking distance, and a wood duck nest box project begun in 1974 now has an average of forty hens successfully nesting in a five-square-mile area centered around his studio.

Dr. Nielsen's photography has appeared in virtually every North American outdoor and nature publication, plus numerous calendars, posters, books, advertisements, and sportswear products. He is the author of three previous books with Voyageur Press, *Wild Ducks Postcards, Songbirds Postcards,* and *A Season with Eagles,* which *Country Living* magazine called ". . . spellbinding." Eighteen limited-edition lithographs have been produced, of which fifteen are sold out. His work "Exploding into Spring" has sold over 57,000 prints in an open-ended edition, with the original being purchased for a five-figure sum that rivals the highest price ever paid for a photograph.

Since 1988, Nielsen has been the assignment photographer for Ducks Unlimited, an international organization dedicated to preserving and restoring the world's wetlands and their associated wildlife.